Me
and my
Grandma

Written by Helen Exley and
Illustrated by Jane Massey

My Grandma is kind and soft and gentle.

No one else is so kind,

not anyone in the whole wide world.

She's never cross. She loves me.

a gift for us to share

to:

....

from:

....

OTHER HELEN EXLEY GIFTBOOKS IN THIS SERIES:

Me and my Mum

Me and my Mom

Me and my Dad

Me and my Grandpa

Me and my Friend

Me and my Teacher

OTHER HELEN EXLEY GIFTBOOKS:

Giggles: A Joke Book

Crazy Kids' Jokes

To a lovely Grandma

Published in 2006 by Helen Exley Giftbooks in Great Britain, and Helen Exley Giftbooks LLC in the USA.

12 11 10 9 8 7 6 5 4 3 2

Illustrations © Jane Massey 2006
Copyright © Helen Exley 2006
The moral right of the author has been asserted.

ISBN 978-1-90513-065-8

A copy of the CIP data is available from the British Library on request.

Printed in China

Helen Exley Giftbooks, 16 Chalk Hill, Watford, Herts WD19 4BG, UK,
www.helenexleygiftbooks.com

We talk for hours. Boy, can we talk.

It takes <u>hours</u> to eat

because we tell each other everything.

She wants to know what I've done.

I tell her my troubles

and she's the one person in the world

with time to listen

to everything I need to say.

Grandmas are supposed
to grow slow and old,
but mine doesn't think so.
Her white hairs have
all gone and she says
she's just starting on
the best bits of life now.
She says she's an Adventurer
— I'm going to be one, too.

When we go shopping my Gran buys me anything I want so I don't dare say when I like something. She shops and shops and we walk and walk and laugh and laugh. Back home she flops down and says "My feet are killing me" and "Ah! Tea at last!"

Grandma calls me "Little One"

and silly things like that.

And she never thinks

I can do anything wrong.

She knows absolutely everything

about me and my family.

She keeps every note I ever write.

My Grandma's home smells lovely. Every time I walk through the door she's been baking things for me. I'm the one who's allowed to lick the mixture off the cake spoon. "Thank you, Grandma. They're my best cakes because they're made by you."

Grandmas are supposed to be polite
and quiet and ladylike. But mine's
just not like that. When we went
on the bumper cars she bumped everyone
in sight and shouted her head off.
She was the naughtiest and the noisiest.

When I told her I was making something just for her she started to cry.

She also cries when we say goodbye.

Grandmothers are like that, you know.

My Grandma has an important job.

She is always busy and works very hard.

She looks after other people in her job.

She's got time to help everyone

— especially me.

She never forgets to speak to me on my birthday.

When my best Ted was run over (by our car)

he was badly wounded and torn.

So Grandma mended him, washed him,

and put him out to dry.

She always helps me. Always.

When I have a worry, Grandma can quietly talk it through.
She wants to help me to grow up to be a nice person. Most of all she teaches me about being kind.

If I had everything in the world

I'd give my Grandma a field of poppies.

I love her so much.

And inside me I know that she'll love me,

forever.

WHAT IS A HELEN EXLEY GIFTBOOK?

Helen Exley Giftbooks cover the most powerful of all human relationships:
the bonds within families and between friends, and the theme of personal values.
No expense is spared in making sure that each book is as meaningful
a gift as it is possible to create: good to give, good to receive.
You have the result in your hands. If you have loved it – tell others!
There is no power on earth like the word-of-mouth recommendation of friends!